STEM Projects in **MINECRAFT®**

The Unofficial Guide to MINECRAFT® Zoology

JILL KEPPELER

PowerKiDS press.

Published in 2025 by The Rosen Publishing Group, Inc.
2544 Clinton Street, Buffalo, NY 14224

First Edition

Editor: Greg Roza
Book Design: Rachel Rising
Illustrator: Matias Lapegüe

Photo Credits: Cover, pp. 1, 3–24 Soloma/Shutterstock.com; pp. 4, 6, 8, 10, 12, 14, 16, 18, 20 Levent Konuk/Shutterstock.com; p. 5 caneraydin/Shutterstock.com; p. 13 Steve Boice/Shutterstock.com; p. 17 Mark Caunt/Shutterstock.com; p. 19 ArnPas/Shutterstock.com.

Library of Congress Cataloging-in-Publication Data

Names: Keppeler, Jill, author.
Title: The unofficial guide to Minecraft zoology / Jill Keppeler.
Description: Buffalo : PowerKids Press, [2025] | Series: STEM projects in Minecraft | Includes index.
Identifiers: LCCN 2024003945 (print) | LCCN 2024003946 (ebook) | ISBN 9781499447057 (library binding) | ISBN 9781499447040 (paperback) | ISBN 9781499447064 (ebook)
Subjects: LCSH: Minecraft (Game)–Juvenile literature. | Animals in video games–Juvenile literature. | Zoology–Juvenile literature.
Classification: LCC GV1469.35.M535 K467 2025 (print) | LCC GV1469.35.M535 (ebook) | DDC 794.8/5–dc23/eng/20240213
LC record available at https://lccn.loc.gov/2024003945
LC ebook record available at https://lccn.loc.gov/2024003946

Manufactured in the United States of America

CPSIA Compliance Information: Batch #CSPK25. For further information contact Rosen Publishing at 1-800-237-9932.

Contents

An Animal Kingdom

Just like the real world, a *Minecraft* world is full of animals. And just like the real world, these animals fit in many different groups! They all have different **habitats**, different foods they eat, and different ways of interacting with players. They may be different shapes or colors in different places.

Zoology is the scientific study of animal life. You can practice zoology in *Minecraft* too! Learning more about the game's animals can help you survive, explore, and learn more about the world. There are two main kinds of real-world animals: vertebrates (which have a backbone) and invertebrates (which don't). Both kinds exist in *Minecraft* too.

MINECRAFT MANIA

In the real world, there are far more kinds of invertebrates than there are vertebrates. About 95 percent of animals are invertebrates! However, it's the opposite in *Minecraft*. Most *Minecraft* animals are in the vertebrate group.

The creators of *Minecraft* often add new animals and other mobs and features when the game is updated. What do you think will be next?

No Backbone!

Real-world invertebrates can be creatures with soft bodies and no legs, like sponges. They can be mollusks, which may have soft bodies but hard shells, or **arthropods**, which include insects and spiders. There are many other kinds as well.

Minecraft has versions, or types, of bees and silverfish, which are real-world insects. In-game bees are like the real thing in many ways. Silverfish, however, are counted as monsters and not animals! They'll attack you if they can. *Minecraft* spiders and cave spiders are much bigger than real spiders. They're also monsters. The game also has squids that swim in rivers and oceans and drop ink.

MINECRAFT MANIA

Most animals in *Minecraft* are mobs. "Mob" is short for "**mobile** object." Some invertebrates in the game based on real-life animals, however, are just blocks in the game. These include corals, sponges, and sea pickles.

There are two kinds of *Minecraft* squids: regular and glow. They can't live out of the water.

A Mammal Mob

Most animals in *Minecraft* are examples of real-world mammals. A mammal is a warm-blooded animal whose babies drink milk and whose body has hair or fur. Most mammals live on land, but some live underwater and must surface to breathe. *Minecraft* has one **aquatic** mammal: the dolphin.

Mammals are adaptable. They can live in many different places. In *Minecraft*, this is true as well. There are **domesticated** mammals that may live with humans (or *Minecraft* players) and provide services or **resources**. There are wild mammals that can be hostile to players in certain cases. You can **breed** some mammals to get baby animals.

MINECRAFT MANIA

Minecraft mobs, including animals, can be hostile, passive, or neutral. Hostile mobs will always attack players. Passive mobs will never attack. Neutral mobs will attack in certain cases.

Dolphins swim in groups called pods in both the real world and *Minecraft*. Players will get a speed boost when swimming with dolphins.

On the Farm

You can create a *Minecraft* farm to help you get resources. *Minecraft's* versions of domesticated mammals include cows, sheep, horses, donkeys, mules, pigs, cats, and dogs. Cows will give you milk if you have a bucket. Sheep provide wool. Cows, sheep, and pigs all provide meat.

Horses, donkeys, mules, camels, and llamas can all provide **transportation** for players. To tame most of these, keep trying to ride them until they stop bucking you off! Feeding them will make this easier. Camels are always tame in the game. Wolves (dogs) and cats, when tamed with their favorite food, will follow a player.

MINECRAFT MANIA

Wolves are wild and neutral mobs until a player feeds them enough. Tame them with bones. After that, you can feed them cooked or raw meat. Tamed wolves have collars.

Camels spawn in desert villages. Two players can ride them at once. Real Arabian camels also have one hump. They've been used for transportation for thousands of years.

Wild Ones

The wild mammals in *Minecraft* include dolphins, foxes, goats, ocelots, pandas, polar bears, rabbits, bats, and wolves. Only wolves can be tamed. Players can gain the trust of foxes and ocelots. Baby foxes trust a player if the player breeds them from adult foxes. Ocelots will trust a player if fed enough raw fish.

The different animals spawn, or appear, in different biomes. For example, goats appear in mountainous areas, while pandas live in jungles, especially bamboo jungles. They all have their own patterns of behavior. Often, if you learn more about the real animals, it can help you figure out how the *Minecraft* animals will behave.

MINECRAFT MANIA

Mother polar bears in the real world are very protective of their young. So, it makes sense that adult polar bears in *Minecraft* are hostile if they have a cub with them!

Mountain goats can drop horns. Each one makes a sound that many players can hear. They also will ram other mobs, including players, and blocks.

Feathered Friends

Birds are another kind of vertebrate. In the real world, there are more than 10,000 species, or kinds. Birds live almost anywhere on Earth. They have wings and feathers, though not all can fly. In *Minecraft*, there are only two kinds of birds: chickens and parrots. In-game chickens are common and can be found in grassy biomes. Parrots can only be found in jungles.

Chickens are a very useful mob in *Minecraft*. They drop eggs and can provide meat and feathers. A tame parrot will follow its player and sit on the player's shoulder at times. It will sometimes **mimic** nearby mobs!

MINECRAFT MANIA

You can feed chickens seeds to breed them and get baby chickens. Chickens can't fly, but they also don't take fall damage, or harm. Parrots can be tamed with seeds, although they can't be bred.

Minecraft parrots can come in five different main colors. Real parrots also have many different, often bright, colors.

Something's Fishy!

Fish are vertebrates that aren't mammals and live in water. There are more than 34,000 species! They're the oldest known vertebrates. Like real-world fish, *Minecraft* fish can't survive out of water. However, you can pick up a fish with water in a bucket and move it somewhere else.

In *Minecraft*, there are four main types of fish: cod, salmon, puffer fish, and tropical fish. However, there are many different sizes, shapes, and colors of **tropical** fish. In fact, combinations of these three things can make up 2,700 versions of this kind of fish! There's only one version each of the other three kinds.

MINECRAFT MANIA

Using a fishing rod, you can catch all four main types of fish as an item. You can cook and eat cod and salmon. Puffer fish can be used in **potions**.

Real salmon are large fish that usually live in colder waters. Their meat is a popular food. *Minecraft* salmon are a good in-game food too.

Reptiles and Amphibians

The other two main kinds of vertebrates are reptiles and amphibians. Reptiles have dry, scaly skin and breathe air. They include snakes, lizards, and turtles. Amphibians may live in both aquatic habitats and dry land. They include frogs, toads, and salamanders.

The one *Minecraft* reptile is a turtle or sea turtle. These passive mobs live in beach biomes and swim in oceans. *Minecraft* amphibians are frogs and axolotls. Frogs live in swamps and grow from tadpoles that live in water. Axolotls are salamanders. In *Minecraft*, they are aquatic mobs that live in lush caves and come in five different colors.

MINECRAFT MANIA

Real-world sea turtles will return to the beach where they were hatched to lay their own eggs. *Minecraft* sea turtles that are about to lay eggs will do the same!

Real axolotls are sometimes kept as pets. You can't tame *Minecraft* axolotls, but they may help players fight in the water.

Only in Minecraft

While there are versions of many real-world animals in *Minecraft*, there are also animals that only exist in the game. In the *Minecraft* Overworld, there are mooshrooms, allays, and sniffers. Mooshrooms are mushroom cows that only live in mushroom fields biomes. Allays are flying passive mobs that can collect items for players. Sniffers dig out rare seeds.

Some mobs only live in the **dimension** called the Nether. Nether animals include hoglins and striders. Hoglins look a lot like wild pigs and are hostile. Striders are passive mobs that can walk on lava. If you put a saddle on one, you can ride it!

MINECRAFT MANIA

You can put warped fungus from the Nether on a stick and use it to control a strider. Striders get cold and shiver when they're not in lava, though!

Minecraft hoglins can be very dangerous. They usually spawn in groups. When killed, they drop pork chops!

Glossary

aquatic: Living in or spending much time in the water.

arthropod: An animal that lacks a backbone and has a skeleton on the outside of its body, such as an insect, spider, shrimp, or crab.

breed: To bring a male and female animal together so they will have babies.

dimension: A level of existence.

domesticated: Bred and raised for use by people.

habitat: The natural home for plants, animals, and other living things.

mimic: To copy the way something looks, acts, or sounds.

mobile: Able to move.

potion: A drink meant to have a magical effect on someone.

resource: Something that can be used.

transportation: A way of traveling from one place to another.

tropical: Warm and wet.

For More Information

BOOKS

Clarke, Ginjer. *The Fascinating Animal Book for Kids*. Emeryville, CA: Rockridge Press, 2021.

National Geographic Kids. *Cutest Animals on the Planet*. Washington, D.C.: National Geographic, 2021.

Random House. *Minecraft Official Animals Sticker Book*. New York, NY: Random House Books for Young Readers, 2020.

WEBSITES

Animal Types
kids.nationalgeographic.com/animals
National Geographic Kids has many articles about different kinds of animals.

***Minecraft*: The Best Animals to Tame (and How to Tame Them)**
gamerant.com/minecraft-best-animals-how-tame/
GameRant provides information on *Minecraft's* domesticated animals.

Why Can't Every Animal Be a Pet?
kids.nationalgeographic.com/animals
Wonderopolis talks about domesticated animals and exotic pets.

Index